PONIES
at play

PONIES
at play

Sophie Bevan

photography by Alan Williams

RYLAND
PETERS
& SMALL
LONDON NEW YORK

DESIGNER Pamela Daniels

EDITOR Sharon Cochrane

LOCATION RESEARCH Emily Westlake

PRODUCTION Gavin Bradshaw

ART DIRECTOR Gabriella Le Grazie

PUBLISHING DIRECTOR Alison Starling

First published in the United States
in 2005
by Ryland Peters & Small, Inc.
519 Broadway, 5th Floor
New York, NY 10012
www.rylandpeters.com

10 9 8 7 6 5 4 3 2

ISBN 1 84172 857 8

Printed in China

contents

small beginnings

A towering fine-boned Thoroughbred?
An all-powerful shire horse? Or an agile and
speedy quarter horse? No, thanks. A pony
wins every time. When it comes to strength,
character, fearlessness, and downright sass,
nothing beats our diminutive equine friends.

measuring up

So, when is a horse a pony, and a pony a horse? The official word is that size matters. A pony must measure 14.2 hands or less from ground to shoulder. Ponies, being ponies, have dug their hooves in and resisted modernization, being measured still by the width of a hand (4 inches/10 cm).

But there's more to being a pony than simply fitting the height requirements. As any pony-lover knows, a pony has an intellect, character, and bravery that far outweigh his size.

starting out

The horse is a relatively new kid on the block—the story begins with the pony, some 55 million years ago, when a small mammal set primitive hoof on the soil of what is now the United States. *Hyracotherium* or "dawn horse," a 12-inch (30-cm) tall "pony," had arrived. Slowly, it trotted its way across the land bridge, which is now the Bering Strait, into Asia and Europe. By the time man appeared on the scene, some 50 million years later, it had grown into *Equus*, a 13-hand pony.

It wasn't long before the pony caught man's eye, and his imagination, as he etched images onto the walls of his cave during the early dawn of civilization, some 30,000 years ago.

harnessing the pony

The long and successful alliance between man and pony
began about 6,000 years ago on the wild steppes of Eurasia.
But pony power didn't really take off until the invention
of the wheel and the arrival of the chariot. Egyptian,
Babylonian, and Assyrian cultures embraced this equine
ally enthusiastically, breeding larger and stronger types,
from which the horse was born.

My dear madam, you need not
be anxious about the children;
my old Merrylegs will take as
much care of them as you or
I could; I assure you I would
not sell that pony for any money,
he is so perfectly good-tempered
and trustworthy.

ANNA SEWELL,
BLACK BEAUTY, 1877

Mane, forelock, and tail are triple gifts
bestowed by the gods upon the "equus" for the
sake of pride and ornament.

XENOPHON (C. 431–354BC),
ON HORSEMANSHIP

good neigh-bors

A pony is a fine ally to have. These four-legged
friends have been man's companion, at work
and at play for thousands of years. They will toil
all morning in the fields, carry their masters
across hills all afternoon, and still have energy
for some mischief before nightfall!

When it comes to hard work, don't be fooled into thinking that the pony is a pushover. If he thinks he can run rings around you—prepare to be sent into a spin!

A pony's respect is hard earned, and all the more valuable for it. Your trusty steed will literally jump high walls for you, gallop that extra mile when you ask—and expect nothing more than a kind word and his keep in return.

Though patience be a tired mare,
yet she will plod.

WILLIAM SHAKESPEARE,
HENRY V, 1599

The pony followed his master like a dog, and ... would trot off without a whip or a word, and rattle down the street as merrily as if he had come out of the queen's stables.

ANNA SEWELL,
BLACK BEAUTY, 1877

from flight to fight

Although some can be a little high spirited, ponies are not aggressive animals. This is a passive creature who, through his honest, hardworking character, has been led by man into the fiercest battles and the heaviest harnesses. When it came to working down in the mines, his bigger, stronger cousin, the horse, was no use—only the pony was a perfect fit.

pit ponies

No amount of training could prepare these brave animals
for the descent into the noisy darkness of the mine shafts.
The pit ponies' drivers were often young boys, and in the
long days spent together in black tunnels, firm friendships
developed between these unlikely co-workers. Pit ponies
are credited with saving many miners' lives. It was believed
that the animals had a sixth sense, refusing to enter shafts
where just moments later the ceiling would fall in.

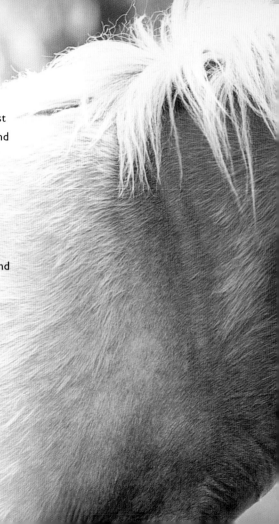

pony power

If you're looking for the strongest pony in the pack, the tiny Shetland wins every time. While a draft horse can pull his own weight, this whizz kid from the Scottish Highlands can drive double the weight of his stocky little frame.

In 1820, a 37-inch (95-cm) Shetland is recorded to have carried a 170-lb. (80-kg) man for 40 miles in one day. The Shetland pony is the original all-terrain quadbike!

It is not enough for a man to know how to ride; he must know how to fall.

MEXICAN PROVERB

horseplay

While the pony makes a great friend, you should be prepared for his wicked sense of humor. It seems that the shorter his legs, the greater his appetite for mischief—as anyone who's ever tried to get the better of a Shetland pony will tell you!

pony baloney

For a naturally shy creature, the pony can be surprisingly
gregarious—even attention seeking. He may leap into the
air if a plastic bag so much as rustles in the hedge, but he'll
also kick on his stable door all morning if he thinks he may
be missing out on any fun and games around the yard.

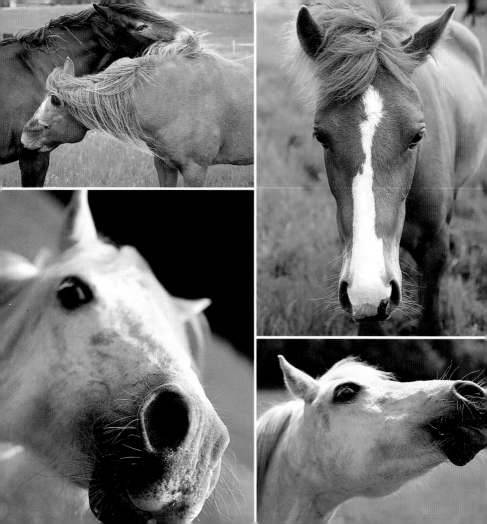

Ponies love to play—unfortunately, their hapless owners are often the butt of the joke! Perhaps your pony has decided that he's carried you far enough, and that a thorny bush looks like just the place to deposit his precious cargo. Or perhaps he'd rather have a game of chase through the lush spring grass than come for a ride at all.

Sure never were seen two such beautiful ponies;
Other horses are clowns, but these macaronies:
To give them this title I'm sure can't be wrong,
Their legs are so slim, and their tails are so long.

RICHARD BRINSLEY SHERIDAN,
THE SCHOOL FOR SCANDAL, 1777

body language

A herd of ponies has complex social dynamics—who gets their food first, who's allowed to nuzzle whom, and who dishes out the discipline. Ponies communicate through body posture, and their ears and lips are often good indicators of what's going on in their heads. Ears pinned back is a sign that the pony is angry or submissive, while a stallion will curl back his lips and pucker up to signal his amorous intentions!

A young animal who steps out of line is swiftly punished with an angry head movement, a nip, or gentle kick. The youngster will then lay back his ears and open and shut his mouth repeatedly, signalling his submission.

[The ponies] would commit some one of the thousand ... tricks which seem to be all a pack-pony knows.

THEODORE ROOSEVELT,
HUNTING TRIPS OF A RANCHMAN, 1885

stable mates

Ponies are sociable creatures and need companionship if
they are to thrive. In the wild, they live in herds, where one
stallion will have a number of mares, but domestic ponies
are no less dependent on each other. If there are no other
ponies or horses to befriend, a pony can also form strong
bonds with other domestic animals. Sheep can make loyal
field mates, and it's not so unusual to see an apprehensive
nanny goat waiting for her pony companion to return from
a ride. Or, if there's really no one better about, a pony will
even humor a little human company!

pony tales

Ponies come in many different guises—from
sure-footed mountain steeds battling
through the winter weather, to polished
gymkhana champions adorned with rosettes.
But what they all have in common is
a personality the size of a carthorse!

Within the shadow of a lonely elm tree
The tired ponies keep.
The wild land, throbbing with the sun's hot magic,
Is rapt as sleep.

HAMLIN GARLAND,
THE UTE LOVER, 1899

wild horses

Wild breeds all over the world have been influenced by the hand of man. In North America, the pony was extinct until the Spanish settlers reintroduced the animal to the continent, where it now roams in vast "wild" herds. In the Welsh hills, Arab stallions were released to improve the native stock, and their fine features can be seen in today's Welsh mountain pony.

My beautiful, my beautiful!
That standest meekly by,
With thy proudly arched and glossy neck,
and dark and fiery eye!

CAROLINE SHERIDAN NORTON (1808–1877),
THE ARAB'S FAREWELL TO HIS STEED

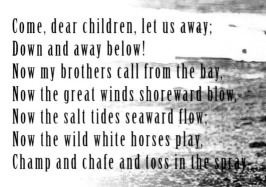

Come, dear children, let us away;
Down and away below!
Now my brothers call from the bay,
Now the great winds shoreward blow,
Now the salt tides seaward flow;
Now the wild white horses play,
Champ and chafe and toss in the spray.

MATTHEW ARNOLD,
THE FORSAKEN MERMAN, 1849

sea horses

On the islands of Chincoteague
and Assateague off the Virginia
and Maryland coasts, there lives
a mysterious pony population.
Not native to the islands, no one
knows how these tiny ponies
came to be there. Legend tells
that they swam ashore from
a shipwrecked Spanish galleon and
came to enjoy island life. Surviving
on a diet of seaweed and shore
grasses is believed to have stunted
their growth.

Every year, ponies are rounded up
on Assateague and swim across
the straits to the main island of
Chincoteague to be auctioned.

well shod

For a lump of iron and a handful of nails, the horseshoe has gained a status far beyond the sum of its parts. For many, it is a symbol of luck and a talisman to ward off evil spirits. According to legend, St. Dunstan was given the task of shoeing the Devil's hoofed feet, but he burned the Devil with his iron and made him promise never to enter a place where a horseshoe was displayed.

However, some horseshoes are more valuable than others. Those used in the stables of the Emperor Nero were made of silver, and the Empress Poppaea shod her mules in gold!

whinnying ways

Ever since the sea-god Poseidon created the horse, it has
been honored, perhaps above any other creature. An
eighteenth-century French prince, Louis-Henri de Bourbon,
built a vast chateau in Chantilly solely to house his prized
horses and ponies. Little has changed today—consider the
price paid for fine polo ponies or for paintings of elegant
steeds which adorn the walls of the fanciest homes.

Last but not least—what greater testament is there to the power of a pony than the girlish bedroom transformed into pony-mad temple, where our four-legged friend adorns everything from wallpaper to stationery?

So, what does the pony think of his elevated status? Does he realize how prized he is? Of course he does! This wise and noble beast was around for millions of years before man, and he'll still be roaming hillsides for many years to come. As anyone who's ever ridden a mountain pony will tell you—this animal will never put a foot wrong.

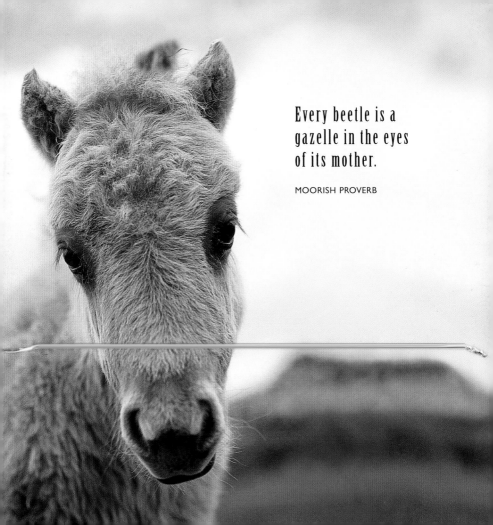

Every beetle is a
gazelle in the eyes
of its mother.

MOORISH PROVERB

acknowledgments

The publisher would like to thank Shirley and Terry Jones, Sue Courtney and Danny Wallace, Shirley and Simon Young, and Lindy Woodhouse, who kindly allowed us to photograph their wonderful ponies.

Many thanks also to our models Katherine Aburrow, Toby Liddiard, Amy Bridgett, Jack Reeves, Chloe Sansom, Daniel Sansom, and Simon Eric Young.

An enormous thank you to Margaret Hayles at Fairytale Pony Farm for all her kind help and advice.

The ponies featured in this book were from the following studs:

Birchcourt Stud
+44 (0)2380 981882
www.birchcourtstud.com
Breeder of Welsh mountain ponies and Welsh ponies of Cob type for show and pleasure.

Pages 4–5, 8 right–9, 13, 15 right, 18 left, 31, 34 left and below right, 38, 40–41, 43, 44 left, 45–55, 60–61, 61 below right

Farriers Stud
Greenacres
New Road
Landford
Near Salisbury
Wiltshire SP5 2AZ
United Kingdom
+44 (0)1794 322821
www.farriersnewforest-ponies.co.uk
farriersnewforest-ponies@sopranet.com
Breeders of stud and forest-bred New Forest ponies.
Simon E. Young
Dip. WCF Farrier

Pages 18 right, 19–25, 32–33, 35–37, 56–59, 61 above right

Golden Oak Miniature Pony Stud
Weston
Berkshire RG20 8JG
United Kingdom
+44 (0)1488 648153
www.goldenoakstud.co.uk
Breeder of Falabella and USA miniature ponies.

Pages 7, 8 left, 26–30, 34 above right, 44 right, 62–63

Maenan Stud
25 Hales Road
Cheltenham
Gloucestershire
GL52 6SL
United Kingdom
+44 (0)1242 573911
www.maenanstud.co.uk
Small stud specializing in breeding show-quality Welsh ponies of Cob type and Welsh mountain ponies.

Pages 1–3, 6, 10–12, 14, 16–17, 39, 41 inset, 42